Quest 3
Pupil's Book

Welcome!
page 2

6 Space Café
page 37

1 The Library
page 5

Revision and Culture
page 43

2 Animal Park
page 11

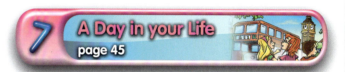
7 A Day in your Life
page 45

3 The Olympics
page 17

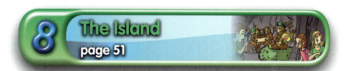
8 The Island
page 51

Revision and Culture
page 23

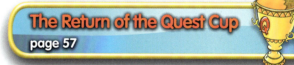
The Return of the Quest Cup
page 57

4 Museum of Natural History
page 25

Revision and Culture
page 60

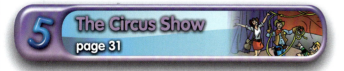
5 The Circus Show
page 31

Festivals
page 62

Jeanette Corbett and Roisin O'Farrell

Welcome!

Lesson 1   1   Listen and read.

2 Investigate and find.
- 3 types of fruit
- 6 types of transport
- 6 animals
- 5 classroom objects

3 **Listen and read. Sing the song.**

Quest School for Investigators.
Welcome everyone!
Explore the world,
collect information
and have lots of fun.

Quest School for Investigators.
Ready 3, 2, 1!
Let's speak English,
work together
and have lots of fun!

Lesson 2 4 Listen to the story. Read. **The Quest Begins**

1. Children, the Quest Cup is very special … Oh no! It's missing!
   The Quest Cup?
   Yes. It isn't here!

2. Mr Fraser, we can find the Quest Cup!
   Look at the symbols on the table. What do they mean?

3. It's a very special table.
   Is the book symbol a library?

4. Children, put your hands on the book symbol. Can you find the Quest Cup?

5. Wow! What's that noise?
   Good luck on your Quest!

Lessons 3 and 4 5 Listen and say the rap.

A is for apple, B is for book, C, D, E, F, G
H is for happy, I, J is for jump, K, L, M, N, O, P
Q is for queen and R is for rap, S, T, U and V
W is for white and window,
X, Y, Zee or Zed.
That's the ABC!
How do you spell cat? C-A-T.
How do you spell dog? D-O-G.
How do you spell rap? R-A-P.
Rapping the ABC!

6 Make your Quest membership card.

Unit 1 — The Library

Lesson 1

1 Listen and read. Sing the song.

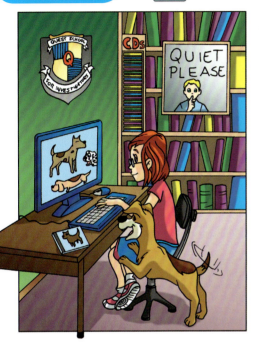

What do you do in the library?
I read books and magazines,
look for information
and watch DVDs.
Every day, for study or play.
I like the library!

What do you do in the library?
I write and listen to stories,
use a computer
and do my homework.
Every day, for study or play.
I like the library!

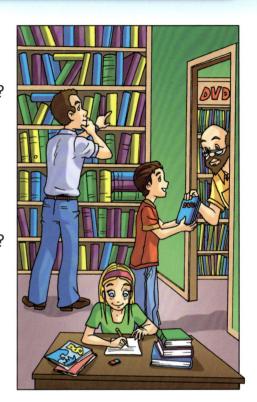

2 Word Quest — Listen and play.

What's this? — Read books.
Yes! What number is it? — Three.

1 listen to stories   2 watch DVDs   3 read books   4 use a computer
5 read magazines   6 look for information   7 do (your) homework   8 write in (your) diary

5

1 The Library — Lesson 2

3 Listen to the story. Read.

Secrets in the Library

4 **Listen and say.**

peacock read tree magazine
music listen Tim sit

Tim and his peacock
sit under a tree.
They listen to music and
read magazines.

1 The Library Lesson 3

5 Listen and read.

6 Let's investigate grammar.

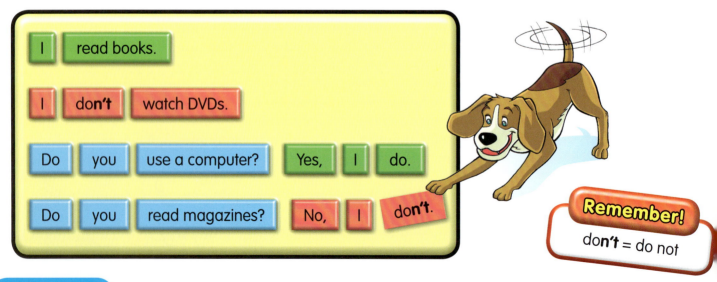

Remember!
do**n't** = do not

Lesson 4 7 Make your cut-out cards (Activity Book page 65). Play a game.

Lesson 5 — The Library 1

8 Listen. Say the words.

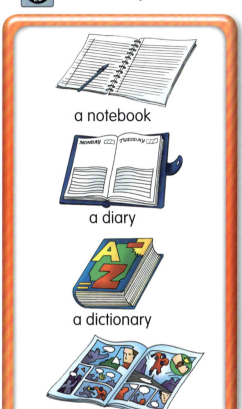

- a notebook
- a diary
- a dictionary
- a comic

9 Listen and read. Say the rap.

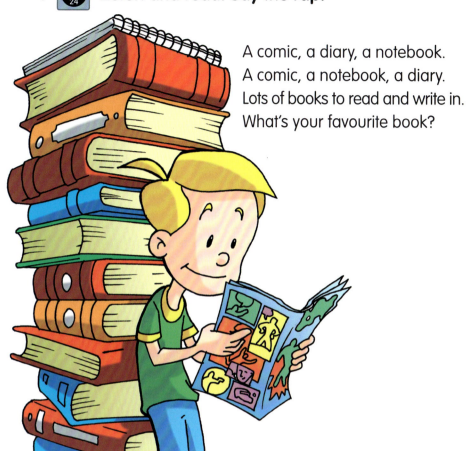

A comic, a diary, a notebook.
A comic, a notebook, a diary.
Lots of books to read and write in.
What's your favourite book?

10 Listen and read.

A Dog's Day

1. "Hello, Scotty! What's that?" "Hi, Yorkie. This is my diary."
2. "What's that?" "This is my dictionary."
3. "This is a comic." "Great pictures!"
4. "This is my favourite story book. It's about a giant." "Oh no!"
5. "Hello!" "Hi, Jack!" "Are you a giant?"

1 CLIL Languages and Literature — Lesson 6

11 Listen and read.

Alphabets by Olga

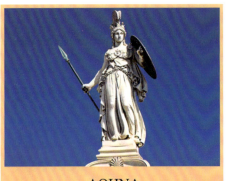

ΑΘΗΝΑ

This is Greek writing. This word means 'Athena'. Greek is a very old language. Some English words come from Greek, for example, 'ASTRONAUT' (ΑΣΤΡΟΝΑΥΤΗΣ). The Greek alphabet is different but some letters are the same. Do you know any other words from Greek?

宮殿

This is Chinese writing. The alphabet is very different. This word means 'palace'. You can read Chinese from left to right, from top to bottom or from right to left. It's very different to English!

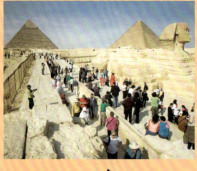

هرم

This is Arabic writing. There are 28 letters in the Arabic alphabet. You read Arabic from right to left. This word means 'pyramid'. How many letters are there in your alphabet?

12 Read and say 'True' or 'False'. Listen and check.

1. Greek is a very old language.
2. The Greek alphabet is the same as the English alphabet.
3. You can read Chinese from top to bottom.
4. There are 26 letters in the Arabic alphabet.
5. You read Arabic from left to right.

13 Listen and learn about an amazing story.

This story comes from Greece. It's called 'The Ant and the Grasshopper'. In the summer the ant works all day collecting corn. The grasshopper plays and in the winter he has no food.
by Charlie

Lesson 7 **14** Do the revision page (Activity Book, page 11).

Lesson 8 **15** Write and draw in your Quest Grammar and Writing Diary.

Unit 2 Animal Park

Lesson 1

1 **Listen and read. Sing the song.**

I like animals!
Different kinds of animals.
Rhinos, cheetahs and tigers, too.
And do you like gorillas?
Yes, I do!

I love animals!
Different kinds of animals.
Whales, dolphins and seals, too.
And do you like kangaroos?
Yes, I do!

2 **Word Quest
Listen and play.**

What's this animal? A tiger.
Yes! How do you spell it? T-I-G-E-R.

1 	2 	3 	4 	5 
6 	7 	8 	9 	10 

1 tiger   2 zebra   3 gorilla   4 cheetah   5 kangaroo
6 bear   7 rhino   8 whale   9 dolphin   10 seal

4 **Listen and say.**

gorilla kangaroo green grapes
jump giraffe oranges
juggles

Gorilla and kangaroo
jump and clap
as giraffe juggles
oranges and green grapes.

2 Animal Park — Lesson 3

5 Listen and read.

6 Let's investigate grammar.

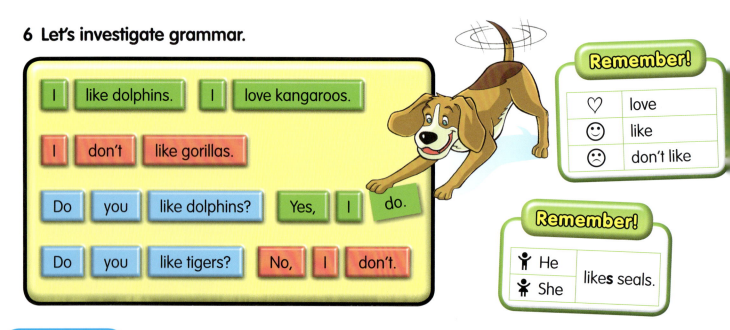

Lesson 4 **7** Make your cut-out cards (Activity Book page 67). Play a game.

Lesson 5 — Animal Park 2

8 Listen. Say the words.

fish
meat
fruit
plants

9 Listen and read. Say the rap.

Let's find out what animals eat.
Dolphins eat fish.
Gorillas eat fruit.
Kangaroos eat plants
and tigers eat meat.
Now we know what animals eat.

10 Listen and read.

A Dog's Day

1. Hello, Scotty.
   Hi, Yorkie. I'm hungry. Let's look for some food.
2. What's that?
   It's fish! Oooh! I don't like fish!
3. Look! Lettuce and carrots.
   No, thank you! I don't like plants.
4. It's a bowl of fruit!
   Gorilla's eat fruit. I'm not a big gorilla!
5. Mmm! This is great! I like meat.
   Hello!
   You're big, Jack. Are you a gorilla?

2 CLIL Natural Science — Lesson 6

11 Listen and read.

Australian animals by Charlie

Red kangaroo

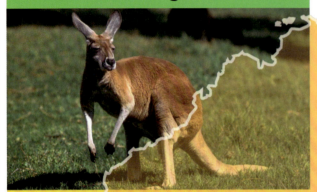

This is a Red kangaroo. It lives in deserts and grasslands in Australia. It lives with other kangaroos in a group. It's called a mob. The Red kangaroo is a herbivore. It eats fruit and plants. It runs very fast, up to 60km an hour. Baby kangaroos stay in the pouch for 235 days. Do you know how many months this is?

Australian dingo

This is an Australian dingo. It's a wild dog. It lives in forests and grasslands in Australia. It lives alone or in a pack with other dingoes. Dingoes are carnivores. They eat other animals. Dingoes make special sounds to communicate, but they don't bark!

12 Answer the questions. Listen and check.

1 Where does the Red kangaroo live?
2 What do you call a group of kangaroos?
3 What does the Red kangaroo eat?
4 Do dingoes eat plants?
5 Do dingoes bark?

13 Listen and learn about an amazing animal.

This is a koala bear. It lives in Australia. It eats eucalyptus leaves. It can eat half to one kilo a day. It sleeps for eighteen hours a day!
by Anna

Lesson 7   14 Do the revision page (Activity Book, page 18).

Lesson 8   15 Write and draw in your Quest Grammar and Writing Diary.

Unit 3 The Olympics

Lesson 1

1 **Listen and read. Sing the song.**

Run, jump, play.
What sports can you do?
I can swim. Splash, splash!
But I can't rollerblade. Zoom, crash!
Can you play basketball?
Yes, I can.
Me too. Me too.

Run, jump, play.
What sports can you do?
I can play tennis. Whack!
But I can't ride a bike. Zoom, crash!
Can you do gymnastics?
Yes, I can.
Me too. Me too.

2 **Word Quest
Listen and play.**

 What's this?  Swim.
Do you swim? Yes, I do.

| 1 play football | 2 run | 3 swim | 4 play tennis | 5 skateboard |
| 6 play basketball | 7 do gymnastics | 8 ride a bike | 9 do judo | 10 rollerblade |

3 The Olympics — Lesson 2

3 **Listen to the story. Read.**

3 The Olympics — Lesson 3

5 **Listen and read.**

6 Let's investigate grammar.

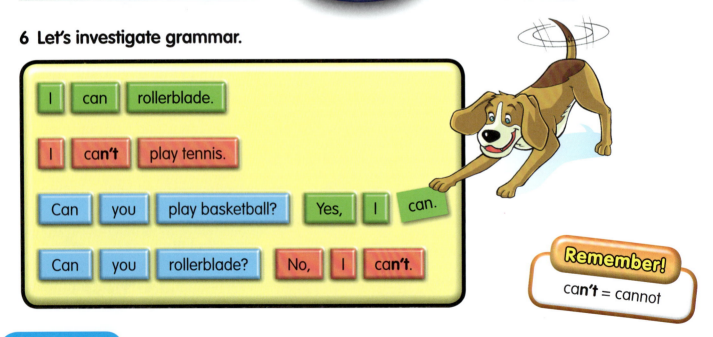

Remember! can't = cannot

Lesson 4 7 Make your cut-out cards (Activity Book page 69). Play a game.

Lesson 5   The Olympics   3

8 Listen. Say the words.

9 Listen and read. Say the rap.

I've got my helmet and trainers.
My goggles and racket, too.
Today I'm feeling sporty.
What sports can I do?

10 Listen and read.

3 CLIL P.E. — Lesson 6

11 Listen and read.

Olympic sports by Anna

Athletics

This is Usain Bolt. He's from Jamaica. He's an Olympic athlete. He runs 100 and 200 metres. He's got a gold medal for running. It's easy to run. All you need are trainers.

Whitewater canoeing

This is David Florence. He's from Scotland. He's got a silver medal for whitewater canoeing in the Olympics. To go canoeing you need a helmet, a life jacket and a canoe.

Cycling
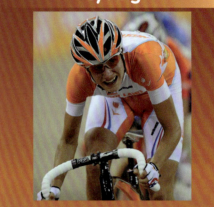
This is Leire Olaberría, an Olympic cyclist. She's from Spain. She's got a bronze medal for the 25km race. To cycle you need a bike and a helmet. Always remember to wear your helmet when you go on your bike!

12 Read and say 'True' or 'False'. Listen and check.

1. Usain Bolt is from England.
2. Usain has got a gold medal.
3. David Florence is from Scotland.
4. David has got a medal for cycling.
5. Leire Olaberría is a cyclist.
6. Leire has got a gold medal.

13 Listen and learn about famous Olympians.

This is Gemma Mengual and Andrea Fuentes. They are synchronized swimmers. They swim underwater with their eyes open.
by Olga

Lesson 7
14 Do the revision page (Activity Book, page 25).

Lesson 8
15 Write and draw in your Quest Grammar and Writing Diary.

Units 1, 2, 3 Quest Revision

1 Read, ask and answer in pairs. Listen and check.

Can you find a black animal?

Yes. A gorilla. It's in A2.

Can you find …?
1 a black animal.
2 something you can ride.
3 an intelligent animal.
4 a sport with a ball.
5 something you can watch.
6 a girl using a computer.
7 something you can read.
8 two big brown animals.
9 a boy with a skateboard.

2 Look at the picture. Find the five letters to make the secret word.

Wildlife in the UK

1 Listen and read. Answer the questions.

Puffins
Puffins can run, swim and fly. They can't climb trees. They eat fish. I like puffins!

Foxes
Foxes can run, jump and swim, but they can't fly. They eat small animals. I like foxes!

Badgers
I like badgers. They eat plants and worms. They can run and jump, but they can't swim or climb trees.

1 Can puffins fly?
2 Can foxes swim?
3 Do badgers eat fish?

2 Your Investigation. Read and write about animals in your country.

Writing plan

Animal: Iberian lynx
Food: meat
What can an Iberian lynx do?
run ✓
climb ✓
jump ✓

♡ love
☺ like ✓
☹ don't like

Iberian lynx
The Iberian lynx eats meat. It can run, climb and jump. I like the Iberian lynx!

Unit 4 Museum of Natural History

Lesson 1

1 **Listen and read. Sing the song.**

A giant body and scary claws.
Let's sing about dinosaurs.

Has it got a tail? Yes, it has.
Has it got wings? Yes, it has.
And it's got a head and eyes, too.
And I can see it looking at you.

A giant body and scary claws.
Let's sing about dinosaurs.

Has it got a mouth? Yes, it has.
Has it got legs? Yes, it has.
And it's got a neck and teeth, too.
And I can see it looking at you.

RUN!

2 **Word Quest**
Listen and play.

What's number 10?

A body.

Can you spell it?

B-O-D-Y.

| 1 wings | 2 a tail | 3 a mouth | 4 teeth | 5 legs |
| 6 a neck | 7 a head | 8 eyes | 9 claws | 10 a body |

4 Museum of Natural History — Lesson 2

3 Listen to the story. Read.

4 Museum of Natural History — Lesson 3

5 Listen and read.

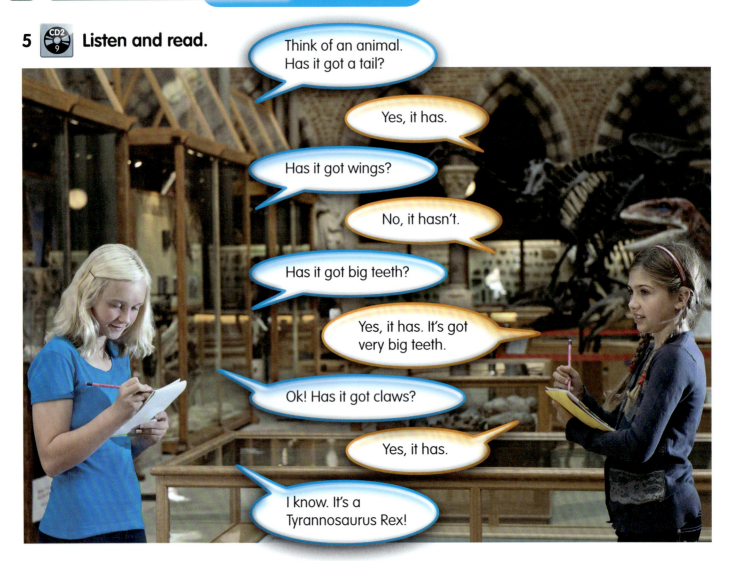

6 Let's investigate grammar.

Remember!
hasn't = has not
it's = it has

Remember!
I've got two legs.
I haven't got claws.

Lesson 4   **7** Make your cut-out cards (Activity Book page 71). Play a game.

Lesson 5 — Museum of Natural History — 4

8 Listen. Say the words.

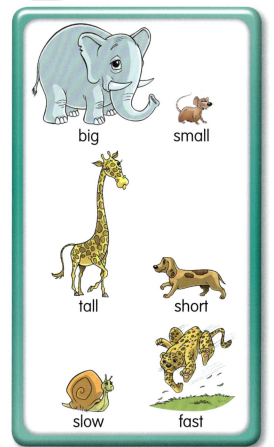

big small
tall short
slow fast

9 Listen and read. Say the rap.

Big or small.
Big or small.
Tall or short.
Tall or short.
Fast or slow.
Fast or slow.
It's got big claws.
It's got big claws.
What is it?
What is it?
It's a dinosaur!
It's a dinosaur!

10 Listen and read.

A Dog's Day

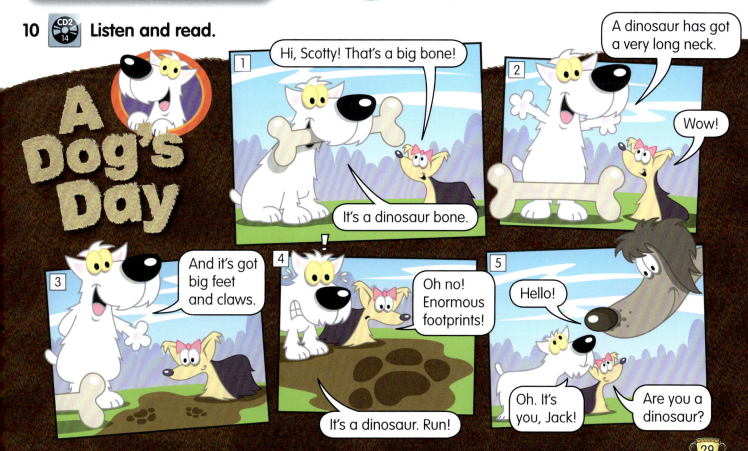

1. Hi, Scotty! That's a big bone! / It's a dinosaur bone.
2. A dinosaur has got a very long neck. / Wow!
3. And it's got big feet and claws.
4. Oh no! Enormous footprints! / It's a dinosaur. Run!
5. Hello! / Oh. It's you, Jack! / Are you a dinosaur?

4 CLIL Natural Science — Lesson 6

11 Listen and read.

Modern day dinosaurs by Olga

The Galápagos tortoise

A giant Galápagos tortoise is about 1 metre tall and about 1.2 metres long. It's very slow. It walks about 200 metres per hour.
It's got a big shell, a small head and four short legs.

The Komodo dragon

A Komodo dragon is 0.75 metres tall and about 3 metres long. It's fast. It runs about 18km per hour.
It's got 60 sharp teeth, a yellow tongue and big claws.

12 Answer the questions. Listen and check.

1. How tall is a giant Galápagos tortoise?
2. How fast can the tortoise walk?
3. Has the tortoise got a big head?
4. How long is the Komodo dragon?
5. How fast can a Komodo dragon run?
6. How many teeth has it got?

13 Listen and learn about an amazing reptile.

This is an alligator snapping turtle. It swims and it walks. It's 66cm long. It's got a shell and a big mouth.
by Charlie

Lesson 7 **14** Do the revision page (Activity Book, page 32).

Lesson 8 **15** Write and draw in your Quest Grammar and Writing Diary.

Unit 5 The Circus Show

Lesson 1

1 **Listen and read. Sing the song.**

Everybody, here we go!
Welcome to the Quest fashion show.

On the left, we see Charlie.
He isn't wearing a coat.
He's wearing a jacket and jeans
and his scarf is blue.
He's wearing cowboy boots, too.

On the right, we see Anna.
She isn't wearing a dress.
She's wearing a shirt and a skirt
and her belt is blue.
She's wearing a cowboy hat, too.

2 **Word Quest
Listen and play.**

What's this? — A dress.
What number is it? — Six.

| 1 boots | 2 jeans | 3 shirt | 4 hat | 5 skirt |
| 6 dress | 7 coat | 8 jacket | 9 belt | 10 scarf |

5 The Circus Show — Lesson 3

5 **Listen and read.**

- Look! There's Lucy Lane and Rob Jackson, the famous actors.
- Where? I can't see.
- There! Lucy's wearing a pink skirt and Rob's wearing a jacket.
- Is Lucy wearing a grey jumper?
- No, she isn't.
- Is Rob wearing a hat?
- Yes, he is.
- Oh yes. I can see now!

6 Let's investigate grammar.

Lucy's / She's — wearing — a pink skirt.

Rob / He — isn't wearing — a blue jacket.

Is Rob wearing a hat? Yes, he is.

Is Lucy wearing a grey jumper? No, she isn't.

Remember!
- He's = He is
- She's = She is
- isn't = is not

Remember!
- I'm wearing a hat.
- I'm not wearing a jacket.

Lesson 4 **7 Make your cut-out cards (Activity Book page 73). Play a game.**

Lesson 5   The Circus Show   5

8 Listen. Say the words.

9 Listen and read. Say the rap.

She's wearing a bracelet.
She's wearing earrings.
She looks cool.
He's wearing a watch.
He's wearing a badge.
He's going to school.

10 Listen and read.

5 CLIL Social Science — Lesson 6

11 Listen and read.

Clothes by Charlie

The climate in the desert is very hot and dry. People wear long clothes to protect them from the sun. He's wearing a long white shirt and a hat. She's wearing a red and white dress and a bracelet.

The climate in the Arctic is very cold and windy. People wear a lot of clothes to protect them from the cold. He's wearing fur trousers and boots. She's wearing a fur coat.

12 Read and say 'True' or 'False'. Listen and check.

1. The climate in the desert is hot and wet.
2. The man in the desert is wearing a white coat and a brown belt.
3. The woman in the desert is wearing a red and white dress.
4. The climate in the Arctic is cold and windy.
5. The man in the Arctic is wearing fur trousers and trainers.
6. The woman in the Arctic is wearing a fur coat.

13 Listen and learn about useful clothes.

This is Daniel in the Australian desert. It's hot. He's wearing a hat with corks. It protects him from flies. by Olga

Lesson 7
14 Do the revision page (Activity Book, page 39).

Lesson 8
15 Write and draw in your Quest Grammar and Writing Diary.

Unit 6 Space Café

Lesson 1

1 **Listen and read. Sing the song.**

I'm so hungry,
I want something to eat!
Do you want to eat sandwiches?
No, I don't.
Do you want to eat chicken?
Yes, I do.
I want to eat chicken.
Mmm, chicken and salad, too!

I'm so hungry,
I want something to eat!
Do you want to eat sausages?
No, I don't.
Do you want to eat meatballs?
Yes, I do.
I want to eat meatballs.
Mmm, meatballs and spaghetti, too!

2 **Word Quest
Listen and play.**

 What's number 3? — It's salad.
Do you like salad? — Yes, I do.

| 1 sandwiches | 2 chicken | 3 salad | 4 sausages | 5 potatoes |
| 6 eggs | 7 meatballs | 8 spaghetti | 9 ice cream | 10 chocolate |

6 Space Café — Lesson 2

3 Listen to the story. Read.

Space Café 6

4 Listen and say.

Charlie cheetah chips lunch
shoes shiny fish

Charlie likes fish and chips for lunch, but his cheetah likes shiny shoes.

6 Space Café — Lesson 3

5 Listen and read.

6 Let's investigate grammar.

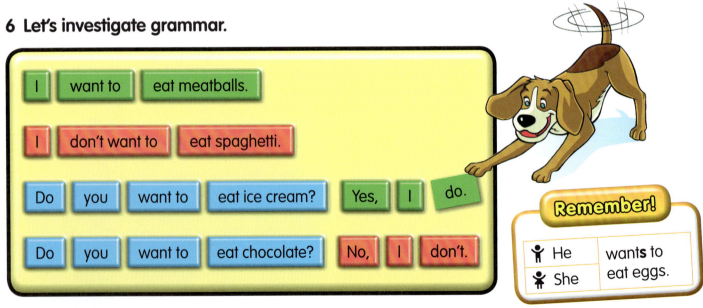

Lesson 4

7 Make your cut-out cards (Activity Book page 75). Play a game.

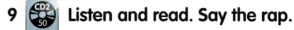

Lesson 5 — Space Café 6

8 Listen. Say the words.

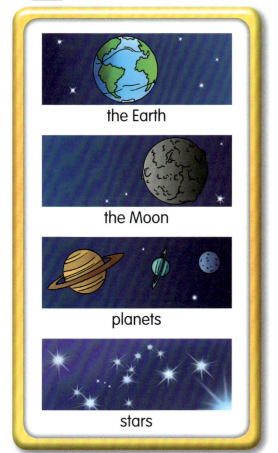

9 Listen and read. Say the rap.

From the Earth, at night, we can count the stars and see the planets and the Moon.
It's daytime now, here comes the Sun.
Goodbye stars, see you soon!

10 Listen and read.

6 CLIL Science — Lesson 6

11 Listen and read.

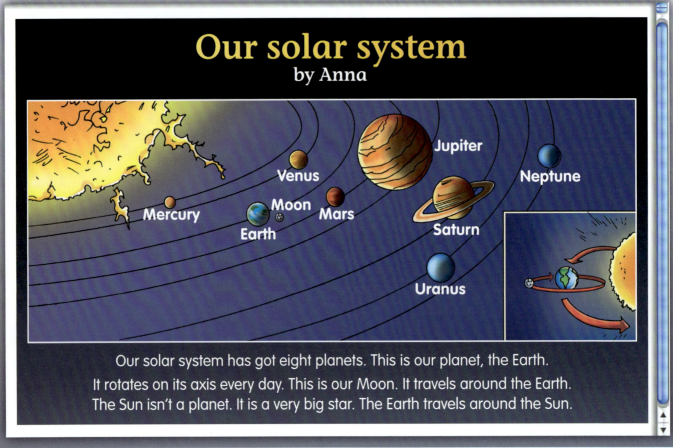

Our solar system
by Anna

Our solar system has got eight planets. This is our planet, the Earth. It rotates on its axis every day. This is our Moon. It travels around the Earth. The Sun isn't a planet. It is a very big star. The Earth travels around the Sun.

12 Read and say 'True' or 'False'. Listen and check.

1. Our solar system has got six planets.
2. The Earth goes around the Sun.
3. The Earth isn't a planet.
4. The Moon travels around the Earth.
5. The Sun is a big star.

13 Listen and learn about the Moon.

This is the Moon. It takes twenty-seven days and seven hours to travel around the Earth. There are mountains and valleys on the Moon. The Moon hasn't got an atmosphere. Do you want to go to the Moon?
by Charlie

Lesson 7
14 Do the revision page (Activity Book, page 46).

Lesson 8
15 Write and draw in your Quest Grammar and Writing Diary.

Units 4, 5, 6 Quest Revision

1 **Read and say 'True' or 'False'. Listen and check.**

1. There's an alien with two mouths and four wings.
2. The woman's wearing trousers and a red scarf.
3. The boy wants to eat sausages.
4. The woman wants to eat spaghetti.
5. The girl's wearing jeans and boots.
6. The red alien has got a short tail.
7. The green alien has got three eyes and three legs.
8. The man's wearing a yellow jacket and a hat.
9. The orange alien wants to eat meatballs.

There's an alien with two mouths and four wings.

True. It's in A2.

2 Look at the picture. Find the eight letters to make the secret word.

Clothes in the UK

1 🎧 **Listen and read. Answer the questions.**

Bridesmaid dresses
The two girls are bridesmaids at a wedding. They're wearing white dresses. They've got flowers in their hair.

Police uniform
The policeman is wearing a uniform and a helmet. It's dark blue. There's a special badge on the helmet.

Kilt
This boy is wearing a kilt. It's a skirt for men. It's different colours. People wear them to parties and weddings in Scotland.

1 What colour are the bridesmaid dresses?
2 What is on the policeman's helmet?
3 What is a kilt?

2 **Your Investigation. Read and write about clothes in your country.**

Writing plan

Clothes: School uniform (shirt, trousers, shoes)
Season: summer
Colour: white, blue, black
Features: badge — symbol of school

♡ love
☺ like
☹ don't like ✓

School uniform
This is David. He's wearing a school uniform. It's his summer uniform. He's wearing a white shirt and blue trousers. His shirt has got a badge — the symbol of the school — on it. His shoes are black. I don't like school uniforms.

44

Unit 7 A Day in your Life

Lesson 1

1 Listen and read. Sing the song.

In the morning,
I get up,
I have a shower
and get dressed.
I have breakfast,
I go to school
and study hard with friends like you.

I study English,
I study Maths.
I have lunch
and play games, too.
Then I go home
and I have dinner.
I go to bed, in my bedroom.

2 **Word Quest** Listen and play.

What's this in English?
Get up.
Yes! What number is it?
One.

| 1 get up | 2 have a shower | 3 get dressed | 4 have breakfast | 5 go to school |
| 6 study | 7 have lunch | 8 go home | 9 have dinner | 10 go to bed |

7 A Day in your Life — Lesson 2

3 Listen to the story. Read.

A Trip to London

A Day in your Life — 7

4 Listen and say.

Ruth boots school two
up but

Ruth gets up, puts on her boots, and reads a book, but she doesn't go to school until two.

7 A Day in your Life — Lesson 3

5 Listen and read.

6 Let's investigate grammar.

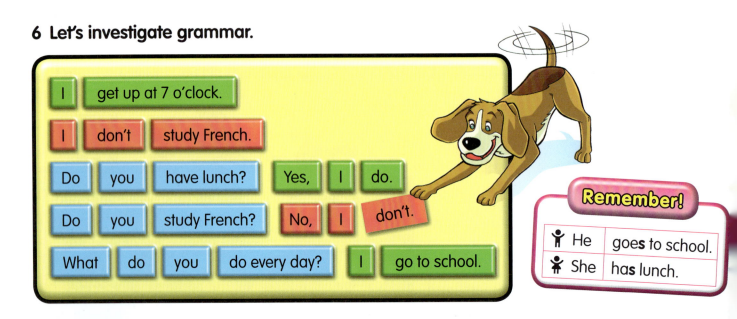

Remember!
He goes to school.
She has lunch.

Lesson 4

7 Make your cut-out cards (Activity Book page 77). Play a game.

Lesson 5 — A Day in your Life

8 Listen. Say the words.

9 Listen and read. Say the rap.

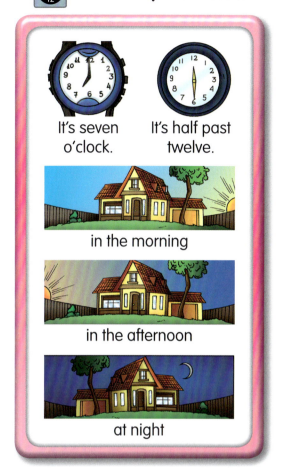

It's seven o'clock in the morning.
It's time to get up, Fred.

It's one o'clock in the afternoon.
It's time for lunch, Fred.

It's half past nine at night.
Why aren't you in bed, Fred?

10 Listen and read.

7 CLIL Social Science — Lesson 6

11 Listen and read.

Time zones by Olga

Olga

Malina

Pablo

Matt

There are different time zones in the world.
In Liverpool it's 7 o'clock in the morning. I'm at home. I get up at 7 o'clock.
In Madrid it's 8 o'clock in the morning. Pablo is at school. He goes to school at 8.
In Sydney it's 6 o'clock in the afternoon. Matt is at home. He has dinner at 6.
In Honolulu it's 9 o'clock at night. Malina is at home. She goes to bed at 9.

12  Read and say 'True' or 'False'. Listen and check.

1. Olga goes to school at seven o'clock in the morning.
2. Pablo lives in Sydney.
3. Matt has dinner at six o'clock.
4. When it's six o'clock in the afternoon in Sydney, it's seven o'clock in the morning in Liverpool.
5. Malina lives in Honolulu.
6. Malina goes to bed at ten o'clock.

13 Listen and learn about daily routines.

This is Molly. She lives in Canada. She gets up at seven o'clock in the morning and has a shower. She has pancakes and maple syrup for breakfast. Maple syrup is very sweet!
by Anna

Lesson 7 — 14 Do the revision page (Activity Book, page 53).

Lesson 8 — 15 Write and draw in your Quest Grammar and Writing Diary.

Unit 8 — The Island

Lesson 1

1. 🎧 Listen and read. Sing the song.

In the middle of the island
there's a big palm tree.
And from the top of that tree,
what can you see?

There's a lake and there's a cave.
There's a river and a beach.
There's a forest and a path.
There's a mountain and a waterfall.

In the middle of the island
there's a big palm tree.
And from the top of that tree,
what can you see?

2. 🎧 **Word Quest** Listen and play.

What's this in English? — A mountain.
Can you spell it? — M-O-U-N-T-A-I-N.

| 1 island | 2 river | 3 lake | 4 mountain | 5 forest |
| 6 cave | 7 waterfall | 8 beach | 9 palm tree | 10 path |

4 🎧 **Listen and say.**

Tom the tig*er* has a show*er* by the riv*er* and aft*er* he has breakfast with his broth*er*.

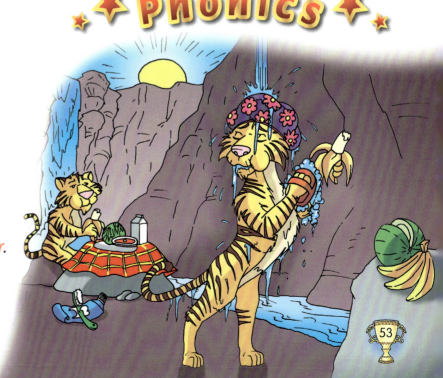

8 The Island — Lesson 3

5 **Listen and read.**

6 **Let's investigate grammar.**

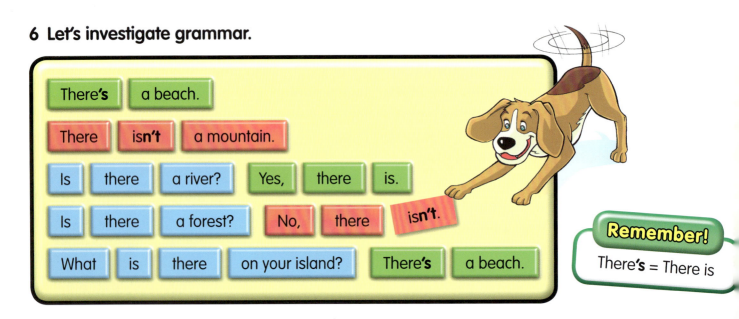

Remember!
There**'s** = There is

Lesson 4 7 **Make your cut-out cards (Activity Book page 79). Play a game.**

Lesson 5 — The Island

8 Listen. Say the words.

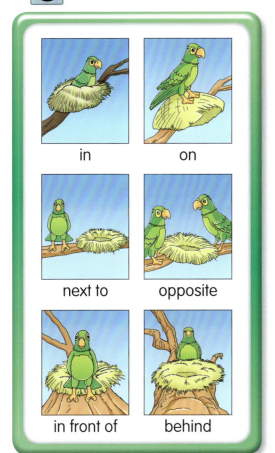

in   on
next to   opposite
in front of   behind

9 Listen and read. Say the rap.

Things in different locations.
What can you find?
On, in, opposite, next to,
in front of, behind.

10 Listen and read.

A Dog's Day

1. Hello, Scotty!
   Hi, Yorkie! Can you help me make my island?

2. There's a lake in front of my forest.
   And there's a beach next to the lake.

3. And look! There's a mountain behind the lake.
   There isn't a mountain!

4. Hello!
   Oh, it's you, Jack!

5. Jack, are you a mountain?
   No, Yorkie. I'm just a very big dog!

8 CLIL Geography — Lesson 6

11 Listen and read.

Islands by Charlie

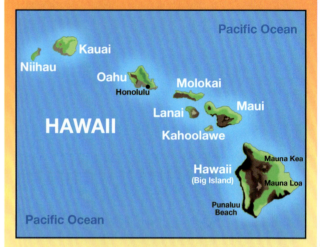

The Isle of Wight is a small English island. There is a river called Medina. You can walk in the beautiful forests on the island. There is a famous boat race from the town of Cowes every year.

This is Hawaii. It has got over 100 beautiful islands made by volcanoes. Hawaii is part of the USA, but it is very far away. The capital is Honolulu. There is a very high mountain. It is called Mauna Kea. Punaluu Beach in Hawaii has got black sand.

12 Answer the questions. Listen and check.

1. Is the Isle of Wight an English island?
2. What is the name of the river on the Isle of Wight?
3. Where is the famous boat race?
4. Is Hawaii one island?
5. What is the capital of Hawaii?
6. What colour is the sand on Punaluu Beach?

13 Listen and learn about an interesting island.

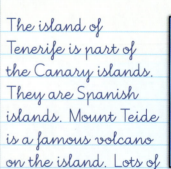

The island of Tenerife is part of the Canary islands. They are Spanish islands. Mount Teide is a famous volcano on the island. Lots of people go to Tenerife because they like the beautiful beaches with palm trees. In Tenerife when it's hot on the beach, it's cold on Mount Teide.
by Olga

Lesson 7 — **14** Do the revision page (Activity Book, page 60).

Lesson 8 — **15** Write and draw in your Quest Grammar and Writing Diary.

The Return of the Quest Cup

1 Do the Quest Cup Quiz.

1 What is the school called?

2 Has Anna got a camera?

3 What animals do the children see in the Animal Park?

4 What is a triathlon?

5 Describe a modern day dinosaur.

6 What is the ringmaster wearing?

7 How many planets are there in our solar system?

8 What time does Anna have lunch?

9 What do you do every day?

10 What is there on the island in the unit 8 story?

2 Look, find and group the things from the stories.

3 🎵 CD3 39 **Listen and read. Sing the song.**

Quest, Quest!
We're Quest Investigators.
Exploring the world
for things that fascinate us.

Do you know things you can do in a library?
And that kangaroos live together in mobs?
An Olympic gold medal means you're number one
and studying dinosaurs is lots of fun.

Quest, Quest!
We're Quest Investigators.
Exploring the world
for things that fascinate us.

Do you know a cowboy wears a hat and boots
and around the world machines give us food?
In London Big Ben is very tall
and you can find the Quest Cup behind a waterfall!

Units 7,8 Quest Revision

1 Read and say. Who says what? Listen and check.

1. I get up at eight o'clock.
2. I play tennis at eight o'clock.
3. There's a fox in the cave.
4. There's a cat behind the tree.
5. I have breakfast at eight o'clock.
6. I get dressed at eight o'clock.
7. There's a waterfall next to the lake.
8. There's a tortoise opposite the badger.

Who says 'I get up at eight o'clock.'?

Mike in A1.

2 Look at the picture. Find the eight letters to make the secret word.

Places in the UK

1 **Listen and read. Answer the questions.**

The Tower of London
This is the Tower of London. People say there are ghosts! It's next to the River Thames. It opens at nine o'clock in the morning.

Buckingham Palace
This is the Queen's home. There's a lake and a big garden. There are a lot of paths. You can visit in the summer.

Madame Tussaud's
This museum is 200 years old. It's got statues of famous people. It opens at nine o'clock in the morning.

1 Is the Tower of London next to a river?
2 What can you see in Madame Tussaud's museum?
3 Is the garden in Buckingham Palace small?

2 **Your Investigation. Read and write about places in your country.**

Writing plan

Place: Oceanographic Aquarium
Where is it? Valencia, Spain
What can you see?
lots of fish and animals from different parts of the world, a dolphin show, an underwater restaurant
What time can you visit?
10 o'clock in the morning

♡ love ✓
☺ like
☹ don't like

Oceanographic Aquarium
The Oceanographic Aquarium is in Valencia, Spain. You can see lots of fish and sea animals from different parts of the world. There is a dolphin show and an underwater restaurant. The Aquarium opens at ten o'clock in the morning. I love the Oceanographic Aquarium.

61

Halloween

1 Listen and read.

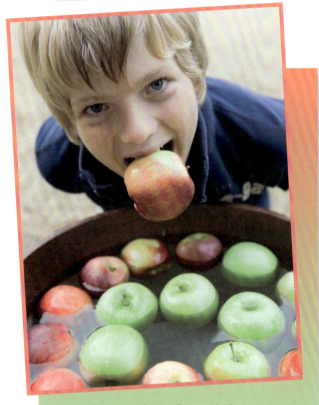

In the USA and the UK, children wear costumes and go 'trick or treating'. People give them sweets. Children carry Jack o' Lanterns. Which costume do you like?

At Halloween lots of people have parties. A traditional game in England is 'apple bobbing'. It's great fun! Can you pick up an apple with your teeth?

A traditional Halloween food in Ireland is Barmbrack. It's sweet bread. You can eat it hot or cold. Delicious! What do you eat at Halloween?

2 Read and say 'True' or 'False'.

1 'Apple bobbing' is a game in the USA.
2 You use your teeth to pick up an apple.
3 People eat sweet bread in Ireland at Halloween.
4 Barmbrack is from England.
5 Children go 'trick or treating' in the USA.
6 They don't wear costumes.

3 Make a Jack o' Lantern.

Christmas

1 Listen to the story. Read.

The Little Donkey

2 **Listen and read about Christmas food.**

Hi! I'm Grace and I'm from England. For Christmas dinner we have turkey and stuffing, sausages, Brussels sprouts and potatoes. For dessert we have Christmas pudding.

I'm Ben from Jamaica. At Christmas we eat goat curry with rice and peas. Mum makes a traditional Christmas cake. It's delicious!

Hello! We're from Australia. Christmas here is in the summer. Some people have a barbecue and eat prawns and seafood on the beach. But we like turkey and mince pies. What do you eat at Christmas?

3 Make a Christmas cut-out.